# Rabbit Hole

Rabbit Hole
© Crystal Ignatowski / Cathexis Northwest Press

No part of this book may be reproduced without written permission
of the publisher or author, except in reviews and articles.

First Printing: 2024

ISBN: 978-1-952869-98-3

Cover Image by Ella Arie
Editing & Design by C. M. Tollefson
Cathexis Northwest Press
cathexisnorthwestpress.com

# Rabbit Hole

Poems by
Crystal Ignatowski

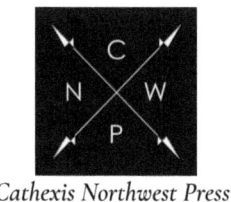

Cathexis Northwest Press

Crystal Ignatowski's *Rabbit Hole* is a two-pronged exploration of its title—the "rabbit hole" is both the endless deep dive into a history and also an Alice in Wonderland-esque entrance into another realm. The speaker of these poems fluctuates between feeling small in moments of shame and feeling large in her remembrance, and in the contrast Ignatowski demonstrates the allure of escaping, how returning to the site of harm might return some of the power we've lost. But sometimes, we go down the rabbit hole because of our need for the familiar; comforts yes, but the old pains we know, too.

~ Taylor Byas, author of *I Done Clicked My Heels Three Times* (2023)


The poems of Crystal Ignatowski's *Rabbit Hole*, spare and dream-like in their details, devastate, operating with the urgency and intimacy of the biographical and of confessional address. One can't help themselves, reading these pages, when they think of the phrase "*born out of necessity.*" Ignatowski confronts here, with daring candor, both the inevitability and plasticity of an individual life, so that naturally, when she writes "*I always wished I had/ the pleasure/ of another name*," one couldn't imagine it written any other way.

~ Edward Sambrano III, poet, critic, and educator

*Rabbit Hole* by Crystal Ignatowski is a spellbinding journey through the surreal and poignant landscapes of memory, identity, and self-discovery. Ignatowski's chapbook weaves imagery and raw emotion to take readers down a path where the ordinary transforms into the extraordinary. From contemplating the anatomy of a name to the hidden spaces within to exploring familial connections and personal trauma, each poem invites introspection and wonder. *There is no single word for the feelings molting / inside me these last five months, sharp as quills—Rabbit Hole* responds to the moment, carries the quiet weight of a gun, and the ephemeral nature of love and loss. These are poems I want to go down the rabbit hole with—I want every reader to dive into this collection and allow yourself to be both lost and found with its lyrical embrace.

~ Kelli Russell Agodon, *Dialogues with Rising Tides* (Copper Canyon Press)


How we name ourselves and how we tell stories, how we cannot stay the same, no matter what befalls or uplifts us, how we bend – these are the emotional tenets of Crystal Ignatowski's *Rabbit Hole*. The poems herein challenge their speakers and their readers to let go, beginning in the shimmering "*uterus of a diamond*" and chasing some version of salvation as light or lineage, as men, as vices, as beauty even, given to us whether we accept it or not. From the absinthe-tinted daydream of the title poem, to the pastoral reverie of "*Quiet Spaces*," the wistful laments of "*Never Have I Ever*" and "*Silo*," Ignatowski's artful lines and lingering images seek both understanding and determination that the journey down, into and through is worth it. And here, in these brilliant poems, it is.

~ Ben Kline, author of *It Was Never Supposed to Be* and *Dead Uncles*

"We're all mad here."

**—Chesire Cat,
Lewis Carroll's *Alice's Adventures in Wonderland***

# Table of contents

| | |
|---|---|
| Uterus of a Diamond | 1 |
| My mother was born in Seoul, South Korea | 3 |
| A Gun Is Not A Father Or A Husband Or A Saint | 4 |
| Rabbit Hole | 5 |
| Sugar Baby | 7 |
| Five Years Later, I'm Commuting to a New Job in Portland | 8 |
| Quiet Spaces | 9 |
| The back room inside Quality Trophy in Salem, Oregon | 10 |
| Bird | 11 |
| Never Have I Ever | 12 |
| Twenty-Twenty | 14 |
| Silo | 15 |
| Notes | 17 |
| Acknowledgements | 19 |

# Uterus of a Diamond

Dying did not hurt. I passed

chevron clouds, licked sugar

from their sides. I witnessed

egrets keep track of the mail.

Once, I forgot how to spell my name.

I followed a hare down a hole.

*Let go of your need*

*to tell a story*, she said, so I did.

I thought about the anatomy of my name,
the uterus of a diamond, what I hid
behind the medicine cabinet mirror.

I swallowed the swallow
who stutters in my garden every morning
just to see what it felt like
to have something inside.

I was born

a million-dollar baby,

a calla lily opening far

too soon for the season, already

naming holes which had no names.

And what came next was

both a swollen blackness

and a space simply waiting

for light.

# My mother was born in Seoul, South Korea

but I never knew her then. Scrawny arms
and porcelain skin. Hair like a loon's nest,
but it wasn't a home yet, she wasn't
a home yet.

It is Mother's Day. We are kayaking.
The sun is hot against our flesh.
Hers is tanning, mine is turning
red.

I ask her if she considers herself
biracial. The question hangs
above our heads. She answers,
but I hear something different:
the story of her green fabric
slippers, her cloth doll friend,
how her mother signed her
adoption papers in red lipstick,
how she signed away
her Kim.

My mother was born in Seoul, South Korea,
but I never knew her then. The tips
of our kayaks glide through the water
like needles with no thread. We are moving
but we leave no trace.

# A Gun Is Not A Father Or A Husband Or A Saint

My father has a gun.
Maybe in his dresser drawer.
Maybe underneath his bed.

Our family doesn't speak of it.
The gun is not meant to kill. We don't
believe in that. I repeat,
We don't believe in that.

My father is away on business, in a suit,
on a plane, in a car, on a train,
with a briefcase full of things. A red
model Cadillac, a poodle made of pearls.

He sleeps in a hotel room.
He makes a human-sized indent
in the bed. My mother is at home alone
with a hidden gun. We've grown used to it.
I repeat, We've grown used to it.

At night we pray. We check our pulses
when we wake. A loaded gun
collecting dust is just a heavy gun,
they say.

# Rabbit Hole

Chase the white
tail. That's what
he said.

Ziplock bag. So tiny.
Dust on a mirror.
Then gone.

Wonderland was.
Many things at once.
But never good.

I still went back
to chase the rabbit.
Every day for a year.

I grew big and then
little and then big
again.

Hats and Cheshire
cats. My life unfolded
like a note.

Every crease:
a line I chose
to cross.

It took years
to fold my life back
into shape.

Origami crane.
Cootie catcher
from fifth grade.

A folded bunny
reminiscent
of the chase.

A geometric
shadow. Darting
on the wall.

My neck
whipping. Bracing
for the fall.

# Sugar Baby

Tacoma was never good
to me, but I was never
good to it. I should have been
in California or Alaska or
New York. Instead, I was in
the house of a stranger, bare
feet on his carpeted stairs, fresh
lemon squeezed in my hair. I was on
the landing, I was in the hallway, I was in
the bedroom, I was in the bed.
The entire time, I stared at
*Thérèse Dreaming* on the wall.
Afterwards, the cash felt thin
like paper because it was.

I always tried to be
quiet in the street the next morning.
I would pull my car door closed
instead of slam it, as if
a different sound
would mean a different
me. My engine would
start the sound of escape,
but there was no escape,
just gray clouds
above a sunken horizon,
over 150 days of rain
a year. I would
always be
back with gritted teeth
and a new black dress,
but the wrong eyes
were seeing it,
seeing me.

# Five Years Later, I'm Commuting to a New Job in Portland

I saw a man on the side of the road with long hair
in unkempt curls. I thought you moved to Sweet Home.
I remember your smile and your white tank tops ripped
at the seams. But mostly I remember your hands on my throat
and how you always carried around a knife. It stuck out your waistband
like a weed. You would come home late and lay all the guns on the bed
like they were our children. *We're all safe*, you would say,
lighting up a cigarette, flicking the ash on the duvet,
*now get naked.* And I would do it, part of me an animal,
part of me already slaughtered. The day I locked the doors
to the house was the day I learned to love the half of me still living.

The man on the side of the road could have been
you, but I was moving fast along the freeway.
When I whisked by, his curls flew up like a skirt caught
in the wind. They stuck to his face so I couldn't
see him. Just his pale neck was visible,

exposed.

# Quiet Spaces

*after Kaveh Akbar*

On the road to Sisters
you opened yourself up
to me. Told me about when
you were eight. Told me about
your cousin Ruth and what your uncle
made you do, what he watched.
This poem is starting itself too soon.

On the road to Sisters
you opened yourself up
to me as I watched balsamroot poke
through gentle snow and ravens land
on dusted pines. The radio
was just low enough to hear
something other than the quiet space
between us. I tried to imagine
you at eight, your body a blank
slate.

Sometimes I forget you
used to be a different person than
the one I sleep next to each night.

On the road to Sisters
you opened up to me.
Afterwards, we talked
about the latest news: black holes
and the woman whose eyes
were filled with bees. It's true:
*the universe has already written*
*the poem you were going to write.*

# The back room inside Quality Trophy in Salem, Oregon

smells like dust. CB draws up the design
and I lower into a swivel chair, turn my head upwards,
spin. It's been years since I was here, sprawled out,
legs wide. He turns the sandblaster on high,
makes a joke about the machine's name
as if it was meant to be. *CrystalBlast 400.*
I spin into the past. I turn twenty-three again:
homeless, spending my days in the shop to keep
warm. *Remember when we had that RV,* CB asks,
and I nod remembering the swollen camper,
its lopsided floor, how we'd lose things
all the time: lighters, pens, cigarettes,
how we'd find them in the corner
days later, how we'd call it *luck.*
But no one called it that
when our friend's parents found Michael days later
in the corner of their own backyard, slumped behind
the dahlias, his head blown off. We attended
the service, wore black, held hands.
I don't remember what was said,
but I remember *Your Hand In Mine*
by *Explosions In The Sky,* how it played
on the radio back to the shop, repeating
and repeating as if caught
in a loop. CB tells me its finished
and I wonder what he's referring to, wonder
if he can see straight through me,
why I've come back after all these years,
freshly married, one kid, and a house.
We're all just freshly married with kids
and houses now. I offer to pay him
but he says it's already paid. The sandblaster
hums itself down.

# Bird

There is no single word for the feelings molting
inside me these last five months, sharp as quills.

I dream of migrating to a wider space. I think of
all the men I've loved, who came inside me

and shouted a version of my name, how none of them
mattered. Like how all the bird feeders in my yard hold

different seed, but every bird that lands is simply *bird.*
I think about the man in my writing group with long hair

and tennis shoes, how I dream of him unzipping me
and letting all my insides out.

Some mornings, I wake in that silent time and listen
to my husband breathe. He is full of trazodone to keep him

down, keep him breathing like a deer in the wild, still
wilding. We said *until death do us part,* but we meant

until it parted us. All the birds fly away in a fluttering
mess when I startle. They mimic what I can't put into words.

# Never Have I Ever

∞

I drive to my high school to see

        if I was always
        this way.

∞

I pass football field bleachers,

        the ones I was never
        kissed under.

Tennis courts I never played on

        because I wasn't gifted

        and I didn't like short skirts.

I pass the auto shop, the class I never took,

        but should have, to prevent
        stranded years.

The side parking lot,

        the one pressed against

        the dilapidated house I never
        visited,

        never got tipsy in
        never played spin the bottle
        during math class,

        never smashed
        my hip bones together with a boy

and later wondered if I was pregnant.

I pass the tall arborvitae

next to the softball field where I never
spit tobacco,

but practiced in my head, my life
its brown arc.

I pass the theater,

where I only was one time:
in a pageant with other girls.

When we changed into
our formal dresses, I watched them tuck
their boobs into their tops like you'd tuck
your children into bed.

I never had this pleasure.

I always wished I had
the pleasure

of another name.

# Twenty-Twenty

It's the first days of the decade and I shouldn't be
left alone. I am strange and foreign in my body.
Driving home from the party, the freeway feels
longer and the city buildings seem taller. We keep
building everything higher, but we aren't any closer to God
than when we're on a bathroom floor weeping about our lives.
You pull on a cigarette and I ask for a drag even though
I haven't had one in four years and suddenly I'm eighteen again
and making poor choices. Some of us are born with chaos
tugging at us like a kite is tugged by the wind: the more you pull,
the higher it climbs. And this is how I found myself
unbuttoning my high collar, letting down my hair. At some point,
everyone wishes they could be a new version of themselves,
mine just comes every day. I dream of old men and new men
and old friends and new friends. I dream of drinking again.
My lies sustain me in the dark. I am unable to be straight
like a needle. It's the first days of the decade and the sun starts
to rise over neon electric signs because no one ever tells the sun
not to rise. I send myself an envelope with this poem inside
and a robin stamps it *Fragile, Do Not Bend.*

# Silo

*after Caitlin Scarano*

I am hardly the same woman. I pass the gap

in the trees where the white silo stood on Perkins,

where the blonde woman's voice said, *It burned down.*

*Nothing left but a circle of cement*, and then, *I like*

*the word herringbone*, as if she were two people,

one body, like me in my early 20's, my mid-

20's, my late-20's too.

I wasn't married then,

but then I was married: a pure crest arch-

way, an unshuttered window, a forest fire

newly contained. I stopped eating

and became my mother,

fulfilled her Korean name: *beautiful silk*

or *beautiful orchid*, both translations

*something that bends.*

Notes

*Quiet Spaces* references a tweet from Kaveh Akbar.

*Twenty-Twenty* uses a phrase from Hala Alyan's poem, *September, a week in.*

Acknowledgements

Thank you to the editors and staff at the following journals who published these poems first, sometimes in other versions: *Barren Magazine (Bird); Bullets Into Bells - Other Voices (A Gun Is Not a Husband or a Father or a Saint); Cotton Xenomorph (Twenty-Twenty); Glass: A Journal of Poetry, (Quiet Spaces); Honey and Lime Literary Magazine (My mother was born in Seoul, South Korea; Sugar Baby; Five Years Later I'm Commuting to a New Job in Portland)*, and *Perhappened Mag (Rabbit Hole)*.

Huge gratitude to C. M. Tollefson at Cathexis Northwest Press for accepting this work and treating it with the utmost care during the entire publication process.

I am beyond grateful to the following individuals who reviewed single poems or this entire manuscript during its various and wild stages: Ben Kline, Caitlin Scarano, Debby Bacharach, Edward Sambrano III, J. L. Wright, Todd Dillard, Ava Williams, Ian Price, Levi Mira, Dave Carrier, Don L. Robinson, Jeremy Hickerson, Pamela Hobart Carter, and Ellen Roberts Young. Extra special thanks to Ben Kline for his dedication and belief in what I couldn't always see.

Many thanks to my professors at University of Puget Sound: Ann Putnam, William Kupinse, and Hans Ostrom. Thank you Hans Ostrom for continuing to be a resource and friend through the years.

Thank you to Poets On The Coast, especially Kelli Russel Agodon and Susan Rich.

My biggest thanks goes to my loved ones who stood by my side when the storylines in these poems were being endured.

And to my husband, whom I love, thank you for continuing to believe in the good parts of me. I love you.

Finally, thank you God.

Crystal Ignatowski's poetry has been featured in *Barren Magazine*, *Four Way Review*, *River Mouth Review*, *Ghost City Press*, *Glass: A Journal of Poetry*, and more. She is a Best of the Net nominee and the recipient of the 2018 Poets on the Coast Fellowship. She lives in Oregon with her husband and children.

# Also Available from Cathexis Northwest Press:

Something To Cry About
by Robert Krantz

Suburban Hermeneutics
by Ian Cappelli

God's Love Is Very Busy
by David Seung

that one time we were almost people
by Christian Czaniecki

Fever Dream/Take Heart
by Valyntina Grenier

The Book of Night & Waking
by Clif Mason

Dead Birds of New Zealand
by Christian Czaniecki

The Weathering of Igneous Rockforms in High-Altitude Riparian Environments
by John Belk

If A Fish
by George Burns

How to Draw a Blank
by Collin Van Son

En Route
by Jesse Wolfe

sky bright psalms
by Temple Cone

Moonbird
by Henry G. Stanton

southern athiest. oh, honey
by d. e. fulford

Bruises, Birthmarks & Other Calamities
by Nadine Klassen

Wanted: Comedy, Addicts
by AR Dugan

They Curve Like Snakes
by David Alexander McFarland

the catalog of daily fears
by Beth Dufford

Shops Close Too Early
by Josh Feit

Vanity Unfair and Other Poems
by Robert Eugene Rubino

Destructive Heresies
by Milo E. Gorgevska

Bodies of Separation
by Chim Sher Ting

The Night with James Dean and Other Prose Poems
by Allison A. deFreese

About Time
by Julie Benesh

Suspended
by Ellen White Rook

The Unempty Spaces Between
by Louis Efron

Quomodo probatur in conflatorio
by Nick Roberts

Suspended
by Ellen White Rook

Call Me Not Ishmael but the Sea
by J. Martin Daughtry

Wild Evolution
by Naomi Leimsider

Coming To Terms
by Peter Sagnella

Acta
by Patrick Wilcox

Honeymoon Shoes
by Valyntina Grenier

Practising Ascending
by Nadine Hitchiner

Home Visit
by Michal Rubin

LA CIUDAD EN TI: THE CITY WITHIN YOU
by Karla Marrufo
Translated from the Spanish by Allison A. deFreese

Resin in the Milky Way
by Amanda Rabaduex

Bone Hunting
by Trinity Catlin

Muskets for the Bear Problem
by Andrew Whitmer

Self-Portraits as a Reddening Sky
by Samuel Gilpin

Desert
by Eric Larsh

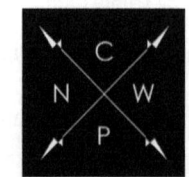

*Cathexis Northwest Press*

www.ingramcontent.com/pod-product-compliance
Lightning Source LLC
Chambersburg PA
CBHW060543080526
44586CB00012B/842